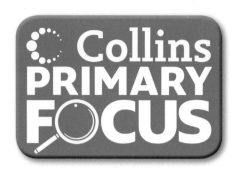

Comprehension
Pupil Book 3

John Jackman

William Collins' dream of knowledge for all began with the publication of his first book in 1819. A self-educated mill worker, he not only enriched millions of lives, but also founded a flourishing publishing house. Today, staying true to this spirit, Collins books are packed with inspiration, innovation and practical expertise. They place you at the centre of a world of possibility and give you exactly what you need to explore it.

Collins. Freedom to teach.

Published by Collins
An imprint of HarperCollins*Publishers* Ltd.
77–85 Fulham Palace Road
Hammersmith
London
W6 8JB

**Browse the complete Collins catalogue at
www.collinseducation.com**

Text © John Jackman 2011
Design and illustrations © HarperCollins*Publishers*
2011

Previously published as *Collins Primary Comprehension*, first published 1998; and *Collins Focus on Comprehension*, first published 2002.

10 9 8 7 6 5 4

ISBN: 978-0-00-741062-0

John Jackman asserts his moral right to be identified as the author of this work.

British Library Cataloguing in Publication Data
A Catalogue record for this publication is available from the British Library.

Cover template: Laing & Carroll
Cover illustration: Steve Evans
Series design: Neil Adams and Garry Lambert
Picture research: Gill Metcalfe
Illustrations: Meena Arnold, Maggie Brand, Rob Englebright, Andrew Midgley, Rhiannon Powell, Peter Bull, Shirley Chiang, Bridget Dowty, Michael Foreman, Kevin Hopgood, Gwyneth Williamson, Rosemary Woods

Acknowledgements
The author and publishers wish to thank the following for permission to use copyright material:
The Random House Group Ltd and Rob Childs for an extract from 'The Big Match' by Rob Childs in *The Big Football Collection* Corgi Childrens, 1995. Reproduced with permission from The Random House Group Ltd and the author Rob Childs; Philip Osment for an extract from *The Lost Gardens*, Collins Education, 2011, reproduced with permission of the author; Lord Alfred Douglas Literary Estate for the poem *The Shark* by Lord Alfred Douglas, copyright © Lord Alfred Douglas Literary Estate; Aitken Alexander Associates Ltd for an extract from *The Borrowers* by Mary Norton, first published by J.M. Dent and Sons Ltd, copyright © Mary Norton, reproduced with permission from Aitken Alexander Associates Ltd; David Higham Associates Limited for an extract from "A Nasty Smile" in "Snakes and Ladders" by Michael Morpurgo from *Three for Tea*, Egmont, 2006. Reproduced by permission of David Higham Associates Ltd; David Higham Associates Limited for the poem "Colonel Fazackerley" by Charles Causley, from *Collected Poems for Children*, Macmillan, 2000. Reproduced by permission of David Higham Associates Ltd; and David Higham Associates Ltd for an extract from "I Go Chicken-Dippy" by Anne Fine, from *The Chicken Gave it to Me*, Egmont, 2007. Reproduced by permission of David Higham Associates Ltd.

Artwork pp40, 41, 47, 48, 49 © Rosemary Woods
Artwork pp11, 12 © Michael Foreman

Every effort has been made to trace copyright holders and to obtain their permission for the use of copyright material. The author and publishers will gladly receive any information enabling them to rectify any error or omission in subsequent editions.

Photographs
p19: VirtualSilver/Alamy; p62: Photodisc/Photolibrary; p63: Jim West/Alamy; p64: Jim West/Alamy

Printed and bound by Printing Express Limited, Hong Kong.

Contents

The Big Match

Danebridge Primary School's football team are leading 3–2 against Shenby School when disaster strikes!

The cup match became an exciting end-to-end battle as the teams threw everything they had left at each other and both goals survived narrow squeaks. Time was rapidly running out, though, for Shenby when they forced Chris to tip the ball round the post for yet another corner and Tim signalled everyone back into the penalty area to protect their slender lead.

The winger played a neat short-corner before whipping the ball across into the box through a great ruck of bodies. It suddenly loomed up in front of Duggan who reacted by blocking it with his hand in panic before a Shenby player could get at it.

As he booted it away, the Shenby team and their supporters were already loudly demanding a penalty for hand-ball and he slumped to the ground in distress.

"It was an accident, I didn't mean to," he pleaded, shaking his head and failing to find any excuse for his stunned team-mates. "I don't know why I did it – it just happened…"

The referee had no choice but to award a penalty and all their hard work seemed to be wasted. Duggan's eyes were not the only ones to be fixed on the goalkeeper Chris in the desperate hope that he could yet somehow rescue the situation.

The spectators grew hushed in anticipation of the duel, the final shoot-out, and some of the players grouped around the edge of the area hardly dared to watch as the Shenby captain prepared to run in to take the penalty.

Duggan stood, head bowed, hoping for a miracle.

Grandad removed the pipe from his mouth, moistened his lips with his tongue and said a little silent prayer.

Mr Jones wiped his hand nervously down his face as the suspense and tension mounted.

But they could do nothing more to help. It was simply all up to Chris.

Rob Childs

Do you remember?

Write a sentence to answer each question.

1. Who was Danebridge's goal-keeper?
2. Who was Danebridge's captain?
3. Which team played the ball into the box from a short-corner?
4. Why was it a bad day for Duggan?
5. Who took the penalty?

More to think about

1. Find these phrases in the passage, and explain them in your own words.
   a) when disaster strikes
   b) a great ruck of bodies
   c) both goals survived narrow squeaks
   d) rescue the situation
   e) Time was rapidly running out
   f) hushed in anticipation
   g) their slender lead
   h) hoping for a miracle
2. Write a sentence to answer each question.
   a) Why was it an important match?
   b) Why did Duggan touch the ball?
   c) How do we know Duggan was deeply upset?
   d) Why did some of the players hardly dare to watch when the penalty was being taken?

Now try these

1. Write a few sentences describing how you imagine the story finishes.
2. How would you have felt, and what thoughts would have been going through your mind, if you were:
   a) Duggan?
   b) Chris?
   c) Grandad?
   d) the Shenby team captain?
3. Duggan and Chris loved football. It was their favourite game. Do you have a favourite sport? Give your reasons. If you don't like any sports or games, say why.

The Donkey

I saw a donkey
One day old,
His head was too big
For his neck to hold;
His legs were shaky
And long and loose,
They rocked and staggered
And weren't much use.

He tried to gambol
And frisk a bit,
But he wasn't quite sure
Of the trick of it.
His queer little coat
Was soft and grey,
And curled at his neck
In a lovely way.

His face was wistful
And left no doubt
That he felt life needed
Some thinking about.
So he blundered round
In venturesome quest,
And then lay flat
On the ground to rest.

He looked so little
And weak and slim,
I prayed the world
Might be good to him.

                              Anon

Do you remember?

Write the correct answer to each question.

1. How old was the donkey?
   a) one day   b) one week   c) one month

2. What were his legs like?
   a) strong   b) shaky   c) muscular

3. What did he do when he stood up?
   a) ate and drank   b) tried to gambol   c) stood still

4. What did his face look like?
   a) miserable   b) happy   c) wistful

5. How did he lie on the ground to rest?
   a) flat   b) sitting up   c) curled round

More to think about

1. Write the words that are used to describe:
   a) the donkey's legs.
   b) how he tried to move.
   c) what his coat was like.
   d) the expression on his face.

2. Write a definition for each of these words. Use a dictionary to help you.
   a) gambol
   b) wistful
   c) blundered
   d) venturesome
   e) quest

Now try these

1. Do you think the poet describes a young donkey well? Explain your answer.

2. When the donkey is one year old it will be very different. Describe what the donkey will look like and how it will behave.

3. Write the words and phrases you might use to describe these features of a large bull.
   a) his legs
   b) how he moves
   c) his coat
   d) the expression on his face

Unit 3

A Clever Way to Catch a Thief

This is an old tale about a rich man who finds that he is constantly losing things from his house. He suspects that one of his servants may be stealing, but which servant, and how can he be sure to catch the thief?

One evening, when it was getting dark and the servants had finished their day's work, he brought them all together.

"Sadly," he said, "we seem to have a thief amongst us, but with your help I think we can rid ourselves of him or her." The servants looked at each other, sorry to think that one of their number was untrustworthy, but uncertain how the rich man could possibly detect the culprit.

"I have placed a table in the centre of the room next door, and on the table is a box. I have put into the box an old cockerel that possesses magic powers. In turn I want each of you to go into the room. It is dark in there, but don't put on any light. Feel your way to the table and gently rest your left hand on the box."

"But what will that show?" asked one of the servants, quite perplexed.

"If you are not the guilty one, nothing will happen – but if you are the thief, the magic cockerel will immediately detect this and will crow so loudly we shall all immediately hear, and know who is to blame."

The servants glanced at each other, some thinking the rich man might be going mad! Other servants were anxious, not sure whether the cockerel really did possess magic powers. What might happen to them, they thought, if left alone in the dark room with the strange creature?

"If you are innocent you have nothing to fear," reassured the rich man.

So, one by one, the servants went into the room, but not a sound was heard. Not once did the magic cockerel crow.

"Excellent!" exclaimed the rich man as the last servant emerged from the dark room. "Now we know for sure who is the guilty person."

The servants were totally puzzled.

"There is a very good reason why the cockerel made no sound. There was no cockerel in the box to make a sound! Each of you now show me your left hand. There was no cockerel, but there was soot on top of the box," said the man. "You," he exclaimed, thrusting his finger towards the only servant with a clean hand, "must be the guilty person. You were the only person frightened to place your hand on top of the box!"

Do you remember?

Copy these sentences. Choose the correct ending to finish each sentence.

1. The rich man thought his things were being stolen by
   a) a burglar who had broken in.
   b) one of his servants.
   c) the gardener.

2. The servants were
   a) sorry to think one of them was untrustworthy.
   b) cross that the rich man suspected them.
   c) sure they knew who had stolen the goods.

3. The rich man told his servants
   a) to go together into the darkened room.
   b) to go one at a time into the darkened room.
   c) not to go into the darkened room.

4. Inside the room there was
   a) an empty box on the table.
   b) a box on the table with a cockerel inside.
   c) a policeman.

5. The box was
   a) painted black.
   b) covered in black soot.
   c) covered with a black cloth.

More to think about

1. Here are the answers to five questions. Write the question for each one. The first one has been done to help you.
   a) The rich man realised some of his things had been stolen.

   ### Why did the rich man suspect his servants of stealing?

   b) He made each servant in turn go into the darkened room and touch the box.
   c) Not a sound was heard in the room.
   d) There was nothing in the box.
   e) The servant with the clean hand was guilty.

2. Copy these lists next to each other. Draw a line between the words or phrases that have similar meanings. The first one has been done to help you.

   detect — cried out
   culprit — guilty person
   perplexed — find out
   guilty — straight away
   immediately — uneasy
   anxious — not guilty
   innocent — pushing
   thrusting — puzzled
   exclaimed — committed an offence

Now try these

1. Write a brief version of the story in no more than 40 words.

2. Write some sentences to answer each question.
   a) This story took place many years ago. Do you think this method of detection would work now? Explain your answer.
   b) If the events in this story happened now, and you were a police officer, how would you set about solving the crime?

3. Imagine that you were one of the servants. Would you have touched the box? Explain your answer.

Unit 4

The Lost Gardens

This play is set in a restored garden at the beginning of the 21st century, and then in the same garden at the beginning of the 20th century.

SCENE 1

(An Old Lady sits sleeping in a wheelchair.)
(sound effect: birds singing)

MAYA: *(offstage)* Jack! Through here.

JACK: *(offstage)* Where are you?

MAYA: *(offstage)* Over here.

(Maya enters and sees the Old Lady.)

OLD LADY: *(waking)* Ahhhh! There you are at last.

MAYA: Pardon?

OLD LADY: I've been waiting for you. Where are your friends? Jack and Emmy? Do you like the gardens? You know in the old days there were plants from all over the world here? People used to come especially to look at them.

MAYA: Yes, Miss Dickinson told us.

OLD LADY: But then the gardeners left and the family who owned the house moved away and the gardens were forgotten.

(Jack enters holding a map of the gardens.)

JACK: I think we've lost her.

OLD LADY: Ah, there you are, Jack.

(Jack looks up, surprised.)

MAYA: How do you know our names?

OLD LADY: I know everything. You're here with your school to look at the lost gardens. Now isn't it time you went and found the tropical garden?

JACK: What tropical garden?

OLD LADY: It's through there.

JACK: It's not on the map.

OLD LADY: That's because it hasn't been found yet.

(Emmy enters.)

EMMY: You're in trouble. We're not supposed to go off on our own.

OLD LADY: Ah, here she is.

EMMY: Who's she?

(The other two shrug.)

EMMY: She must live in the big house. It's a home for old people. Miss Dickinson said. She looks ancient.

MAYA: That's rude.

OLD LADY: That's all right, my dear. You're having a difficult time at the moment, aren't you, Emmy? Anyway I *am* ancient. It's true. Now the tropical garden's waiting for you. It's just the other side of the brambles. It used to be called the jungle.

EMMY: Cool.

JACK: It's not on the map.

OLD LADY: Where's your spirit of adventure? Now, you'll need this. There's a gate.

(She hands Jack a huge rusty key.)

OLD LADY: Go on. Take it.

(Jack takes it.)

OLD LADY: It's that way.

JACK: Thanks. Come on, Maya.

MAYA: Goodbye.

(Jack and Maya start to go.)

OLD LADY: But you can't leave without Emmy.

JACK: Oh … well …

OLD LADY: Yes?

MAYA: She doesn't really like the same games as us.

EMMY: Yes I do.

OLD LADY: Take her with you.

EMMY: I don't want to spoil their fun.

OLD LADY: You have to stay together.

(Jack looks at Maya. She shrugs.)

JACK: OK. Come on, Emmy.

OLD LADY: Goodbye, my dears. Be careful of the brambles.

(They go. The Old Lady sleeps.)

Philip Osment

12

Do you remember?

1. Write a sentence to answer each question.
   a) Why are the children in the gardens?
   b) Who is Miss Dickinson?
   c) What does the old lady give to Jack?
   d) Why are the gardens overgrown?

2. Read these sentences about the story. Write 'true' or 'not true' for each one.
   a) The elderly lady was sleeping in her wheelchair.
   b) The children were expecting to meet the old lady.
   c) The old lady seemed to know a lot about the children.
   d) She was the grandmother of one of the children.
   e) Maya and Jack get on very well together.
   f) The teacher had told the children to look for the tropical garden.
   g) Emmy was concerned that they didn't get lost.
   h) The old lady had a key to the gate.

More to think about

1. Write a sentence to answer each question about the old lady.
   a) How do we know that she was expecting the children?
   b) Why did Jack look surprised when she first spoke to him?
   c) How do you think she might have known about the tropical garden?
   d) What did she mean when she asked Jack, "Where's your spirit of adventure?"
   e) What do you think of the old lady? Explain how you feel about her.

2. Emmy says that the old lady looks "ancient". Write a list of other things you would describe as "ancient".

Now try these

1. There could be several ways that the story develops.
   Make notes of two different versions of what could happen.

2. Use one of your sets of notes from question 1 to help you write the next scene in the play.

3. There are lots of historical sites all around the world. For example, there is a large garden near Heligan in the south-west of England, now called 'The Lost Gardens of Heligan', that became completely overgrown and has been rediscovered and restored. Research 'The Lost Gardens of Heligan', or a different historical site, and prepare a presentation about it.

Shen Nung

China's age of the 'Great Ten' was when each of ten successive emperors brought new skills and knowledge to this great civilisation, but none more so than Shen Nung. Some legends say he had the head of an ox, but the body of a man.

Being part ox led him to invent the plough, which in China was always pulled by oxen. He showed his people how then to sow seed and cultivate crops. He also taught them how to tame the forests and turn thickly overgrown woodlands into productive land. If they felled the trees in a small area and burned the stumps, they could plant their crops more easily. The ash would enrich the soil, helping their crops to grow well.

Shen Nung is also remembered as the god of medicine. He showed the people which plants would heal them when they were sick. According to the stories he was said to have a see-through stomach which enabled him to watch what was happening inside his body as he ate strange plants. One day he boiled some rare leaves and made a sort of vegetable stew. He drank the juice he strained from the mix. He had discovered tea!

Another of his useful discoveries was ginseng, a plant whose roots clean the blood of any impurities. It was soon recognised as a tonic, making tired people feel energetic and older people feel younger.

Sadly, Shen Nung grew careless and eventually died after swallowing a strange form of grass that was so sharp it cut his stomach to ribbons. But by then the great Emperor had discovered and invented so much his reputation was certain to live on for generations to come.

But so too was Shen Nung's wife to be remembered. She had mastered the art of breeding silkworms. This is a skill known as sericulture. Silkworms produce a thread that can be woven into silk cloth, for which the Chinese have ever since been renowned. To this day much of the best silk in the world comes from China. Shen Nung's wife was also deified, and became the goddess of housecrafts.

Medicine, tea, farming and fine cloth helped make China into one of the greatest civilisations the world has known – and dating back from a time several thousands of years ago, when people in most Western countries were still living in very primitive conditions.

Do you remember?

Copy these sentences. Fill each gap.

1. _____ was one of China's greatest _____.
2. Some say he had the _____ of an ox and the body of a _____.
3. He taught his people how to cultivate _____ and tame the _____.
4. He also showed them how _____ could heal them when they were _____.
5. Shen Nung boiled some _____ and made _____.
6. His _____ mastered the art of breeding _____.

More to think about

1. Read these sentences. Write 'true', 'false' or 'can't tell' for each one.
   a) China has only ever had ten emperors.
   b) Shen Nung was by far the greatest emperor China has ever had.
   c) All early Chinese emperors were thought to be part animal and part human.
   d) Shen Nung was said to have the head of a man and the body of an ox.
   e) He was able to invent the plough because he was part ox.
   f) According to some stories, Shen Nung had a see-through stomach.
   g) Shen Nung liked tea.
   h) The leaves of ginseng are thought to clean the blood.
   i) Ginseng was also soon recognised as a tonic.
   j) The emperor died when he ate a strange form of grass.

2. Make a list of Shen Nung's achievements, and those of his wife.

Now try these

1. Use a dictionary to find the meaning of each of these words.
   a) successive
   b) productive
   c) enrich
   d) renown
   e) deity
   f) primitive

2. Which parts of this legend do you think are true, and which parts are probably fictional?

3. Of Shen Nung's various achievements, which do you judge to be the most important? Give your reasons.

We are all intrigued by magicians, who seem to be able to perform impossible acts, like pulling white rabbits out of hats and cutting a woman in half. Like all performances, though, a magician's real secret is in rehearsing thoroughly before showing anyone their tricks.

Here is a trick for you to learn. After you have practised thoroughly, try it on your family.

You will need

- several matchsticks
- a handkerchief with hems along the edges

What to do

1. Show the audience a matchstick.

2. Take a clean cotton handkerchief from your pocket, shake it out, showing both sides to prove you are not hiding anything.

3. Wrap the matchstick in the handkerchief.

4. Ask one of your audience to feel the matchstick inside the handkerchief, and to break it.

5. Shake the handkerchief, allowing the unbroken matchstick to fall onto the floor!

The secret

Before you begin the performance, slip a matchstick into the hem of the handkerchief. When you ask someone to break the wrapped-up matchstick make sure that they break the one hidden in the hem (when they feel it, they will think it is the one they saw you wrap into the handkerchief).

It's a good idea to have two or three handkerchiefs with matchsticks already secretly in the hems, as your audience is bound to be flabbergasted and ask you to do the trick again. But don't let them realise that you are changing handkerchiefs, or they may become suspicious!

Do you remember?

Copy this paragraph. Choose a word from the box to fill each gap.

> practise   tricks   women   audience   magician
>
> thoroughly   embarrassed   hats   rabbits   work

Magicians often seem to perform impossible _____1_____.
The most famous tricks are getting white _____2_____ from _____3_____
and cutting _____4_____ in half! If you want to be a _____5_____
the most important secret is to _____6_____ your tricks _____7_____.
If you don't practise, your tricks will not _____8_____ and your _____9_____
will laugh and you will feel _____10_____!

More to think about

1. Read these instructions for the matchstick trick. Copy them in the correct order.

> **Ask someone to break the matchstick in the handkerchief.**

> **Show the audience the handkerchief.**

> **Open the handkerchief and show the unbroken matchstick.**

> **Rehearse the trick thoroughly.**

> **Collect together a handkerchief and some matchsticks.**

> **Wrap the matchstick in the handkerchief.**

> **Show the audience a matchstick.**

2. Which word in the passage means:
   a) fascinated (in the first paragraph)
   b) not possible (in the first paragraph)
   c) practising (in the first paragraph)
   d) hidden (in the last paragraph)
   e) amazed (in the last paragraph)
   f) doubtful (in the last paragraph).

Now try these

1. Imagine you were an audience member watching the matchstick trick. Write a report of the trick from your point of view.

2. Do you know a magic trick? If you do, write the instructions step by step like those for the matchstick trick. If you don't, write instructions to teach a young child how to cross a busy road.

3. Imagine that you really do have a magic wand. You can use it to change three things, but three things only! Write what you will change, and say why.

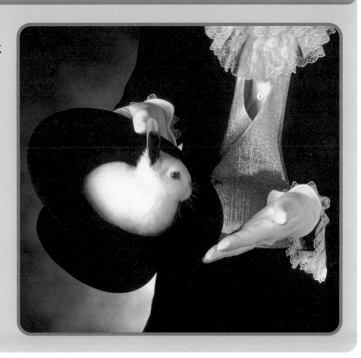

The Shark

A treacherous monster is the Shark
He never makes the least remark

And when he sees you on the sand,
He doesn't seem to want to land.

He watches you take off your clothes,
And not the least excitement shows.

His eyes do not grow bright or roll,
He has astounding self-control.

He waits till you are quite undrest,
And seems to take no interest.

And when towards the sea you leap,
He looks as if he were asleep.

But when you once get in his range,
His whole demeanour seems to change.

He throws his body right about,
And his true character comes out.

It's no use crying or appealing,
He seems to lose all decent feeling.

After this warning you will wish
To keep clear of this treacherous fish.

His back is black, his stomach white,
He has a very dangerous bite.

Lord Alfred Douglas

Do you remember?

Copy these sentences. Fill each gap.

1. The poem is about a _____.
2. He watches as you take off your _____.
3. He pretends to take no _____.
4. The shark even pretends that he's _____.
5. Then suddenly he throws his _____ about.
6. You can see he has a black _____.
7. He has a white _____.
8. He has a very dangerous _____.

More to think about

1. Write one-word answers to these questions in your book.
    a) One word in the poem is not spelt as we would spell it now. Which word is it?
    b) Which word rhymes with sand?
    c) Which word rhymes with asleep?
    d) Which word rhymes with change?
    e) Which word rhymes with appealing?

2. Write a sentence to answer each question.
    a) Why are sharks said to be treacherous?
    b) Explain why the poet says the shark has "astounding self-control".
    c) Why does the shark pretend to be asleep as you run down to the sea?
    d) What is the "true character" of the shark?

3. Write these phrases in your own words. Use a dictionary to help you.
    a) a treacherous monster (line 1)
    b) never makes the least remark (line 2)
    c) not the least excitement shows (line 6)
    d) astounding self-control (line 8)
    e) his whole demeanour (line 14)
    f) throws his body right about (line 15)
    g) his true character (line 16)
    h) all decent feeling (line 18)

Now try these

1. Imagine that you are the shark in the poem. Tell the story in your own words, from the shark's point of view. Start when you are basking in the warmth of the sun, and suddenly you spot …

2. Rewrite the poem as if it were an article for a newspaper.
    The poem doesn't tell us what happened in the end, but your article should.

3. Do you think it is fair to describe all sharks as "treacherous"? Explain your answer. Then make a list of other words you would use to describe a shark.

Southborough Council, High Street, Southborough
Environmental Health Department

Mr J Trigger
Flat 9
High Risings
Hornsey Lane
Southborough

1st October

Dear Sir,

I fear that we have received yet another complaint from one of your neighbours concerning the noise emanating from your home. This is not the first occasion we have had cause to draw this matter to your attention; I refer to my letters of 29th July and 16th August.

On both previous occasions you assured me that the problem would cease forthwith, but those promises appear not to have been fulfilled.

The present complaint refers not only to the volume of the music which you, or other members of your family, are playing from early morning until after midnight, but also to the sound of your dogs constantly fighting, musical instruments being played at loud volumes, and household appliances which I'm informed are in use incessantly.

This letter is our final warning before we shall be forced to take further action to restrain your total disregard for the welfare of your neighbours.

Yours faithfully,

Mr B Quiet
Complaints Officer

Do you remember?

Write the correct answer to each question.

1. Who is this letter from?
   a) The letter is from the Complaints Officer of Southborough Council.
   b) The letter is from Mr Trigger.

2. What is the Complaints Officer's name?
   a) The Complaints Officer is Mr L Noise.
   b) The Complaints Officer is Mr B Quiet.

3. When was the letter sent?
   a) The letter was sent on 1st October.
   b) The letter was sent on 1st December.

4. What is the letter about?
   a) It is about the noise coming from Mr Trigger's flat.
   b) It is about the smell coming from Mr Trigger's flat.

5. Is this the first letter sent to Mr Trigger about noise?
   a) Yes, this is the first letter.
   b) No, there have been other letters sent to him.

6. What happened when the last letter was sent?
   a) When the last letter was sent Mr Trigger made sure all the noise stopped.
   b) Nothing changed when the last letter was sent.

7. What will happen if this letter is ignored?
   a) The Council will take further action if he ignores this letter.
   b) Nothing will happen if Mr Trigger ignores this letter.

More to think about

1. Write a sentence to answer each question.
   a) How many letters has Mr Quiet sent to Mr Trigger?
   b) How did Mr Quiet know a lot of noise was coming from Mr Trigger's flat?
   c) Why is Mr Quiet particularly cross with Mr Trigger?
   d) Does Mr Trigger live alone in the flat?
   e) What are the main causes of the noise?

2. Copy these lists next to each other. Draw a line between each word in the letter to the word or phrase that has a similar meaning. Use a dictionary if you need to. The first one has been done to help you.

Words in the letter	Meanings
emanating	promised
occasion	coming from
assured	constantly
cease	time
forthwith	stop
incessantly	prevent
restrain	lack of consideration
disregard	immediately

Now try these

1. Imagine you are Mr Trigger. You have decided to apologise to your neighbours. Write a letter explaining the causes of all the noise and what you will do to make things better.

2. Write a few sentences to answer each question.
   a) Do you think people should be allowed to make as much noise as they want? Give reasons for your answer.
   b) Has anyone ever really annoyed you in some way? What was the reason, and how was it sorted out?
   c) What things should people be most aware of to prevent upsetting their neighbours?

The Two Brothers

Early one morning two brothers left their village for a hunting trip. They tramped through the hot, parched countryside along dusty paths until suddenly they came across something peculiar.

"What's this? Who can have left this circle of pots standing upside down like this?" said the younger brother.

"Don't touch them," begged the older brother, "I don't like the look of them. I get a bad feeling – just leave them alone!"

"I'm going to take a look," said the younger, braver brother, as he turned over the first pot. Then he did the same to each pot in the line, until, as he turned over the last pot he gave a shout of surprise as out popped a little old woman.

"Don't stand shivering there like a couple of terrified gazelles. I won't hurt you. Follow me, both of you, and I'll show you something really interesting.

But the older brother was rigid with fear, unable to move an inch!

"Coward!" she exclaimed in her tiny, high-pitched voice. But the younger brother, always ready for adventure, followed her, along the tracks and paths until they came to a huge tree.

"Cut this tree down for me," she commanded, but at the first stroke of the axe, to the boy's utter astonishment, out stepped a bullock from a hollow in the side of the tree trunk. Each time the boy chopped at the tree a cow, a bullock, a goat or a sheep came out. Eventually he was surrounded by flocks and herds. "These are for you," the little old woman explained, "for releasing me from that prison."

Thanking the woman, though still almost too stunned to speak, the boy struggled to drive the animals back to where he had left his brother, still rooted to the spot – too scared to move. "Just look what the little old woman gave me! This will make our parents rich, and save our village."

As they drove the animals along the dusty tracks, the boys became increasingly thirsty – and the older brother was quietly wondering how he would cover his shame at his younger brother having been so much braver than he. Then suddenly the older boy saw a stream at the bottom of a ravine. "Look, water! Lower me down with this rope so that I can drink," he said. The younger brother dutifully did as he was asked. When the older brother was back at the top he told the younger brother that now it was his turn to be lowered down. But once at the bottom, the wicked and cowardly older brother saw his opportunity. He tossed down the end of the rope, knowing that he could now take back the animals and be given all the praise from his parents and all the villagers.

Sure enough, when he returned with the herds and flocks to the village, everyone gathered round, singing his praises, fascinated to hear the incredible story of how he came to have been given the animals.
"But where is my younger son?" asked his mother.
"Oh, he went off – alone, he's sure to be back in a few days," lied the older son.

Early the next morning, while the women of the village were collecting water from the well, they heard a honey-bird. Now there were many honey-birds in that part of the country and people had learnt that if they followed the birds they would often lead them to bees' nests where the men could collect supplies of honey. When the women told their menfolk about the honey-bird, several, including the boys' father, followed the bird. Along rough paths, through increasingly dense undergrowth, on and on they ran, pausing only when occasionally the bird settled on a branch or rock for a brief rest. The men became more and more surprised at the distance it was flying.
"That's far enough," said one eventually, "I'm going back."

"Just a little further," said the others. "There could be something very special where the bird is leading us – it seems so determined."

So on they all went, until they came to a precipice, from where, way down below, they could just detect the distant sound of a young boy's voice calling desperately for help. The bird flew straight down into the ravine, landing at the boy's feet. Straining his eyes and ears, the boy's father exclaimed, "My son! That's my son!" The men collected creepers from nearby trees and quickly fashioned a rope, lowering down the father who, having hugged his dear lost son, listened in disbelief at the story his distraught younger son had to tell.
"Alas," wept the father, "that I should have a son so wicked as your older brother. You would have died had not the honey-bird led us to this spot."

But news of the young boy's rescue must have reached home before the men returned to the village, because by the time they did the older boy had left, and was never again seen in the village. But the younger boy prospered and his parents never wanted for anything in their old age.

But to this day no one has ever found the amazing tree or seen the little old woman, though there is one special honey-bird the younger brother feeds every day with seeds and water.

Do you remember?

1. Copy these sentences. Choose the correct word to fill each gap.
    a) The two brothers went _____. (hunting, swimming)
    b) They found a circle of _____. (pots, stools)
    c) The old lady led the younger brother to a _____. (well, tree)
    d) Inside the trunk were many _____. (birds, animals)
    e) The brothers started to drive the animals back to the _____. (village, town)

2. Read these sentences about the story.
    Write 'true', 'false' or 'can't tell' for each one.
    a) The story is about two brothers.
    b) The story is set in America.
    c) The older brother is braver than the younger.
    d) They found a tiny old lady in the trunk of a tree.
    e) She was over 100 years old.
    f) It was hot, and the boys became thirsty.
    g) There was a stream at the bottom of the ravine.
    h) The younger brother trapped his older brother in the ravine.
    i) A honey-bird led the boys' father to the spot.
    j) In the end, the two brothers lived together happily.

More to think about

1. Write a sentence to answer each question.
   a) Why did the older brother not want to touch the circle of pots?
   b) Who was the braver of the two brothers?
   c) How can we tell that the old woman wasn't frightened of the boys?
   d) Why did the woman give the younger brother all the animals?
   e) How do we know it was probably the hot, dry season?
   f) Why did the younger brother give the honey-bird seed and water every day?
   g) What do you think became of the old woman?

2. Find these words in the passage. Write another word or phrase that the author could have used without changing the meaning.
   a) begged
   b) rigid
   c) commanded
   d) ravine
   e) incredible
   f) occasionally
   g) precipice
   h) fashioned

Now try these

1. Write a summary of the story of 'The Two Brothers' in your own words. Your summary should be no more than 60 words.

2. Use the clues in the story, and your imagination, to write short descriptions of the personalities of these main characters:
   a) the younger brother
   b) the older brother
   c) the old lady
   d) the boys' father.

3. What do you think would be the best things about living in a village like the one in the story? What would be the worst things? Make two lists.

4. Write about whether you enjoyed the story. How did it make you feel? What parts did you like most? Did you like the way it was written?

Colonel Fazackerley

Colonel Fazackerley Butterworth-Toast
Bought an old castle complete with a ghost,
But someone or other forgot to declare
To Colonel Fazack that the spectre was there.

On the very first evening, while waiting to dine,
The Colonel was taking a fine sherry wine,
When the ghost, with a furious flash and a flare,
Shot out of the chimney and shivered, 'Beware!'

Colonel Fazackerley put down his glass
And said, 'My dear fellow, that's really first class!
I just can't conceive how you do it at all.
I imagine you're going to a Fancy Dress Ball?'

At this, the dread ghost gave a withering cry.
Said the Colonel (his monocle firm in his eye),
'Now just how you do it I wish I could think.
Do sit down and tell me, and please have a drink.'

The ghost in his phosphorous cloak gave a roar
And floated about between ceiling and floor.
He walked through a wall and returned through a pane
And backed up the chimney and came down again.

Said the Colonel, 'With laughter I'm feeling quite weak!'
(As tears of merriment ran down his cheek).
'My house-warming party I hope you won't spurn.
You must say you'll come and you'll give us a turn!'

At this, the poor spectre – quite out of his wits –
Proceeded to shake himself almost to bits.
He rattled his chains and he clattered his bones
And he filled the whole castle with mumbles and moans.

But Colonel Fazackerley, just as before,
Was simply delighted and called out, 'Encore!'
At which the ghost vanished, his efforts in vain,
And was never seen at the castle again.

'Oh dear, what a pity!' said Colonel Fazack.
'I don't know his name, so I can't call him back.'
And then with a smile that was hard to define,
Colonel Fazackerley went in to dine.

Charles Causley

Do you remember?

Write a sentence to answer each question.

1. What was the Colonel's full name?
2. What did he buy?
3. What did he unexpectedly get with his purchase?
4. When and from where did the ghost first appear?
5. What was the Colonel doing when he saw the ghost?

More to think about

1. Read these sentences about the poem. Copy them in the correct order.

> **The Colonel thought this was really funny.**

> **Colonel Fazackerley bought the castle.**

> **The ghost left, and has not been seen since.**

> **The Colonel joked with the ghost.**

> **A ghost appeared from the chimney.**

> **The ghost became increasingly furious.**

2. Was Colonel Fazackerley frightened of the ghost? What makes you think this?
3. Was the ghost pleased Colonel Fazackerley had bought the castle?
   What did he do to show his feelings?
4. Did the Colonel really want the ghost to stay in the castle?
   Explain your answer.

Now try these

1. What would you have done if you had met the ghost?
2. What sort of person do you think Colonel Fazackerley was?
   Use phrases from the poem to help you answer this question.
3. What does the poet mean when he says at the end of the poem: "And then
   with a smile that was hard to define, Colonel Fazackerley went in to dine"?
4. Do you find the poem funny? Explain your answer, thinking about the poet's
   choice of words and phrases.

A Nasty Smile

The first person Wendy saw at school was Simon McTavish. He was roaring around the playground whirling his bag above his head. Wendy took a deep breath and walked into school hoping he wouldn't notice her.

"Now then children," Mrs Paterson began. "I've had an idea. And where do I always have my best ideas?"

"In the bath," they choroused.

"Quite right," she laughed. "Well now, I was in my bath last night and I was wondering what we should do for the Parents' Evening this Christmas. Year Three are doing the Nativity play this year. Year Four are cooking the mince pies and Year Five are decorating the hall. What shall we do? I know, I thought Year Six will put on an exhibition of 'Interesting Things' in the front hall, so that people will have something to look at while they're eating their mince pies. Well, what do you think?"

Simon McTavish pretended to yawn noisily, but she ignored him.

"Well then, why don't we all try to bring in something interesting, something from the past maybe, something from a far-off country, something amazing, something special."

Mrs Paterson did go on a bit, but Wendy liked her because she laughed a lot.

Sarah said she had a three-legged milking stool. Sharon had a telescope and Vince said he'd bring in a fox's tail.

"And how about you, Wendy?" she said.

There was only one thing Wendy could think of.

"We've got an old war helmet, Miss," she said. "It's my grandad's. He had it in the war. It's a bit rusty though."

"Like your grandad then," said Simon McTavish and everyone sniggered. Wendy felt the tears coming.

"A helmet will be just fine, Wendy," said Mrs Paterson quickly. Then she turned to Simon. "And Simon McTavish, you've got a brain like a soggy Weetabix."

Now they were all laughing at Simon instead, and Wendy suddenly felt a lot better. But for the rest of the day she kept finding Simon McTavish looking at her. There was a very nasty smile on his face.

Michael Morpurgo

Do you remember?

Copy these sentences and finish them in your own words.

1. Wendy was afraid of …
2. Her teacher was …
3. Mrs Paterson had her best ideas …
4. She thought for Parents' Evening her class could hold an …
5. Wendy said she could bring …
6. When Simon McTavish was rude, Wendy …

More to think about

Write some sentences to answer each question.

1. What sort of person was Simon McTavish? Why do you think this?
2. How do we know that Wendy was afraid of him?
3. Why did Wendy like her teacher?
4. If you were Mrs Paterson, how would you have felt about Simon McTavish?

Now try these

1. What do you think happened in the end? Make up your own ending for this story.
2. Turn this extract from the story into a play. Remember to include stage directions to describe the setting, sound effects and actions.
3. If you were being threatened or bullied, write in your book what each of these people would say if you told them.
   a) your teacher
   b) your mum
   c) your grandad
   d) your best friend
4. Write how you would feel, and what you would do, if your younger brother or sister was being bullied or your best friend was frightened of a gang in the playground.

The Borrowers

Kate had sometimes wondered what happens to the little things that go missing. In this extract Mrs May tells her about the Borrowers, tiny people who live in the homes of humans, and borrow what they need to survive.

"I've lost the crochet hook…" (they were making a bed-quilt – in woollen squares; there were thirty still to do), "I know where I put it," she went on hastily; "I put it on the bottom shelf of the book-case just beside my bed."

"On the bottom shelf?" repeated Mrs May, her own needle flicking steadily in the firelight. "Near the floor?"

"Yes," said Kate, "But I looked on the floor. Under the rug. Everywhere. The wool was still there though. Just where I'd left it."

"Oh dear," exclaimed Mrs May lightly, "don't say they're in this house too!"

"That what are?" asked Kate.

"The Borrowers," said Mrs May, and in the half light she seemed to smile. Kate stared a little fearfully.

"Are there such things?" she asked after a moment.

"As what?"

Kate blinked her eyelids.

"As people, other people, living in a house who… borrow things?"

Mrs May laid down her work. "What do you think?" she asked.

"I don't know," said Kate looking away and pulling hard at her shoe button. "There can't be. And yet" – she raised her head – "and yet sometimes I think there must be."

"Why do you think there must be?" asked Mrs May.

"Because of all the things that disappear. Safety-pins, for instance. Factories go on making safety-pins, and every day people go on buying safety-pins and yet, somehow, there is never a safety-pin just when you want one. Where are they all? Now, at this minute? Where do they all go? Take needles," she went on.

"All the needles my mother ever bought – there must be hundreds – can't just be lying around this house."

"Not lying about this house, no," agreed Mrs May.

"And all the other things we keep on buying. Again and again and again. Like pencils and match-boxes and sealing wax and hair slides and drawing pins and thimbles –"

"And hatpins," put in Mrs May, "and blotting-paper."
"Yes, blotting-paper," agreed Kate, "but not hatpins."
"That's where you're wrong," said Mrs May, and she picked up her work again.
"There was a reason for hatpins."

Kate stared. "A reason?" she repeated.
"I mean – what kind of a reason?"
"Well, there are two reasons really.
A hatpin is a very useful weapon and"
– Mrs May laughed suddenly – "but it
all sounds such nonsense and" – she
hesitated – "it was so very long ago!"
"But tell me" said Kate, "tell me how
you know about the hatpin. Did you
ever see one?"
Mrs May threw her a startled glance.
"Well, yes –" she began.
"Not a hatpin," exclaimed Kate
impatiently, "a – what-ever-do-you-
call-them, a Borrower?"
Mrs May drew a sharp breath.
"No," she said quickly,
"I never saw one."

"But someone else saw one," cried Kate, "and you know about it. I can see you do!"
"Hush," said Mrs May, "no need to shout!" She gazed downwards at the upturned
face and then she smiled and her eyes slid away into the distance.

Mary Norton

Do you remember?

1. Write a sentence to answer each question.
   a) What were Mrs May and Kate making?
   b) What had Kate lost?
   c) Where did she think she had put the crochet hook?
   d) Who are the Borrowers?
   e) Where do they live?

2. Read these sentences about the story. Write 'true' or 'not true' for each one.
   a) The crochet hook was missing, but the wool was still there.
   b) Kate told Mrs May about the Borrowers.
   c) Kate wore lace-up shoes.
   d) The little people collected things like pencils, hair slides, drawing pins.
   e) According to Mrs May the Borrowers weren't interested in hatpins.
   f) Mrs May had seen the Borrowers on several occasions.
   g) Mrs May knew someone who had met the Borrowers.

More to think about

1. Write a sentence to answer each question.
   a) Why are the little people called the Borrowers?
   b) What time of the day, and at what time of the year, is the story probably taking place? How can you tell?
   c) How did Kate feel when Mrs May first mentioned the Borrowers?
   d) Why did Kate begin to feel impatient with Mrs May?

2. Make a list of the clues in the passage that tell us that *The Borrowers* was written about 50 years ago.

Now try these

1. Do you think it is possible that there could be tiny people like the Borrowers? Give your reasons.

2. Choose one of the small items mentioned in the passage.
   Imagine that you are a Borrower and write about how you 'borrowed' the item. Explain what you will use it for.

3. Imagine that you were accidentally given a spoonful of medicine that had the unexpected effect of shrinking you. Write about some of the dangers, but also about some of the things you could do if you were tiny.

4. Does this passage from *The Borrowers* make you want to read the whole book? Give your reasons.

Ou and Ouch

There was once a rich farmer who was very wealthy but very miserly. He was always looking for ways of avoiding paying his workers their rightful wages. At the end of each month he would say that they weren't doing their work well enough, and try to make excuses for not paying them all of their money.

One day he hired a young lad who worked hard throughout the month, but when the time came for him to be paid his first wages the farmer said, "Before I can pay you, I need you to go into market to buy me some ou and ouch – and don't come back until you have some."

The other workers looked at each other, for they knew full well the farmer was up to no good. But the boy smiled, undeterred, and walked briskly down the track. He knew about the miserly farmer with his stingy tricks, and so he had a plan.

First, he went back to his old mother's cottage and borrowed two large brown storage jars. "Where are you taking my best brown jars?" enquired his mother. "Don't worry, Mother, I'll bring them back – full of money!"

Next he went into an old shed where he kept his pets – a mouse and a rat! Now, the boy knew that his pets loved him, but he also knew that they did not like being touched by other people. Into one jar he gently put the mouse, and into the other he carefully placed the rat. He put both of the jars carefully into a sack, and off he went back to see the farmer.

"What have you brought!" asked the wizen-faced old farmer, as the other workers looked on quizzically.

"Here is some ou," said the boy, taking the jar with the mouse from the sack.

"How is this ou?" grumbled the gruff, grumpy farmer.

"Open it and you'll see," said the boy.

And no sooner had the old man unscrewed the lid than the mouse had leapt up and taken a firm hold of his finger.

"Ou!" cried out the farmer. "Ou!"

"There, you see," said the boy with a laugh, "and here is a jar of ouch," he added, taking the jar with the big black rat from the sack.

"All right, all right," said the miser, feeling very foolish in front of his workers. "Here are your wages; be off with you, all of you."

But he never tested the jar of ouch, and he never tried to avoid paying his workers their proper wages again.

Do you remember?

Copy this paragraph. Fill each gap.

The farmer was very _____1_____ but very _____2_____. He was always trying not to pay his _____3_____. One day he hired a young _____4_____. At the end of the _____5_____ the boy went to get his wages. The farmer sent him to market to buy some _____6_____ and _____7_____, but instead of going to the market he went home and borrowed two brown _____8_____. He put his pet _____9_____ in one, and his pet _____10_____ in the other.

More to think about

1. Choose words from each column to make five sentences about the story.

Who?	Does what?	When?
The men	never paid his workers	when he returned with the jars.
The farmer	watched the lad	when the farmer sent him to market.
The mouse	thought of a clever plan	when the farmer told the boy to get some ou and ouch.
The workers	bit the farmer's finger	when he opened the jar.
The lad	looked at each other	at the end of the month.

2. Make a list of words that the writer uses in the passage to give us clues about the character of the farmer. Write in your own words what each one means.

3. Why do you think the farmer didn't test the jar of ouch?

Now try these

1. Write a brief version of the story using your own words. Your version should be no more than 40 words.

2. Do you think 'Ou and Ouch' is a good title? Make a list of other possible titles, neatly underlining your favourite.

3. Did you enjoy the story? Write about why you think it was a popular story with farm workers in the past.

4. Has anyone ever tried to trick you or someone you know? Write about what happened.

Robinson Crusoe's Diary

Robinson Crusoe has been shipwrecked on a remote island.

Eighth day   Yesterday I brought back from the ship a quantity of tools, a drill, a dozen hatchets, a grind-stone for sharpening, iron crowbars, a large bag of nails and rivets; with sails, ropes, poles, two more barrels of powder, a box of musket balls, seven muskets, a third shotgun, lead, a hammock, a mattress, blankets, clothes and great-coats. I thought that I had rescued nearly everything that was on board. But I was wrong, for today, returning from a trip to the wreck that almost cost me dear − the wind having risen, I capsized with my whole load in the middle of the creek − I saw Japp, the captain's dog, come bounding joyfully along, an Irish setter I had thought drowned with the crew. I think that the poor beast, swept away by the current, had landed on the island much farther away, and had difficulty in finding me. This evening I pitched a little tent with the poles and sail-cloth, under which I spread my bed. I have piled up all my riches in a shelter from the rain that was threatening. My dog snores at my feet, I have dined on a bit of dried meat and a ship's biscuit, and in spite of a rising wind I am prepared to pass a good night.

Daniel Defoe

Do you remember?

Write the correct answer to each question.

1. How did Robinson Crusoe come to be on the island?
    a) Robinson Crusoe was on holiday on the island.
    b) Robinson Crusoe was bird watching on the island.
    c) Robinson Crusoe was shipwrecked on the island.

2. How long has he been there?
    a) He has just reached the island.
    b) He has been on the island for eight days.
    c) He has been on the island for four days.

3. What happened to the rest of the crew?
   a) The rest of the crew were rescued.
   b) The rest of the crew drowned.
   c) The rest of the crew swam to another island.

4. What pleasant surprise did Robinson Crusoe get on the eighth day?
   a) Japp, the Captain's dog, came bounding along the beach.
   b) He found one of the other crew members alive.
   c) He discovered a sailing boat.

5. Why does he think he will get a good sleep tonight?
   a) He has managed to find a bed.
   b) He has managed to build a tent.
   c) He has managed to find a tin of chocolate.

More to think about

1. List in your book the items Robinson Crusoe retrieved from the wreck.
   Which do you think will be most useful? Explain your answer.

2. Write a sentence to answer each question.
   a) What happened to Robinson Crusoe as he was returning from the shipwreck?
   b) Why was the dog "bounding joyfully along"?
   c) Was Robinson Crusoe pleased with his day's work? Explain your answer.

Now try these

1. In his diary Robinson Crusoe records facts about what he has done, but doesn't
   tell us much about his thoughts. How do you think he would have been feeling?

2. Imagine you are the captain of a ship sailing past the island.
   Describe how you spot Robinson Crusoe and how you rescue him.

3. Think back to one day in your life when something important happened.
   It might be happy or sad, exciting or just unusual. Write a diary entry for that day,
   including details of your feelings and emotions, as well as describing
   what happened.

I Go Chicken-Dippy

I'd never been outside before. Never in my whole life. I went quite silly, really. I feel a bit of a fool even now, thinking back on it. But I went chicken-dippy. I couldn't handle it at all, not everything at once. Not when the only thing I'd known since I was hatched was wire netting and other chickens.

Try and imagine! First, how it felt. All that wet air and wind. I'd never felt wet air ruffling my feathers before. I'd never even been wet. Now here I was staggering about in a slimy mud puddle, stung by fierce little cold raindrops. It was so wonderful! It was like being born again. I felt I'd come alive!

And the noise! Roaring wind. Creaking tree tops. Deafening! The storm sounded like the world cracking in half, just for me, to wake me after a lifetime of having my ears stuffed with chicken cackle. I wanted to do my bit, so I joined in, clucking and squawking like something gone loopy. Being outside in the fresh air was great.

And it was fresh. Fresh and cold. But what I'd never guessed was how many smells go to make up fresh air. Inside the shed was terrible – terrible! Too awful to describe. At the weekends, when we weren't cleaned out, it was even worse. The workers always wore masks, but even so, on some mornings they coughed and choked, and their eyes were red-rimmed. (Imagine how we felt. We'd been in it all night!) Outside, I smelled a thousand things 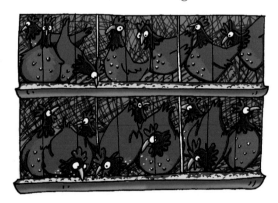 I couldn't even name until later – the leaf-mould underfoot, wet bracken, a thread of exhaust fumes from the road behind, cow parsnip, smoke from the chimney over the hill, the film of oil on the puddles. A giant stew. Smells of the World! And I was breathing it for the first time. Me – a bedraggled middle-aged feather baby.

But I felt *good*.

Anne Fine

Do you remember?

Copy these sentences. Fill each gap.

1. The only thing the chicken had known since she hatched had been other chickens and _____.

2. Even being stung by fierce little cold _____ felt wonderful.

3. The noise the _____ made was deafening.

4. Being outside in the fresh _____ was great.

5. But the chicken had never realised how many different _____ go to make up fresh air.

More to think about

Write some sentences to answer each question.

1. Why is the passage called 'I Go Chicken-Dippy'?

2. Why did the chicken say she couldn't handle it at all?

3. The author has written mostly in short, sharp sentences. Why do you think this might be?

4. Which things do you think the chicken was most pleased to have left behind?

5. What aspects of her new environment did the chicken find difficult to handle at first?

6. What message is the author trying to get across to her readers in the passage?

Now try these

1. Describe a different location from the chicken's point of view. You could choose a house, a shopping centre, a supermarket, a park or somewhere different. How would it look and sound from the chicken's point of view?

2. Imagine that you have had a serious accident and have been told you can't leave your bed for many months. What would you miss most? Think especially of some of the very ordinary things we usually take for granted.
Make a list, and say why you will miss each thing.

3. This passage is from *The Chicken Gave It To Me* by Anne Fine. Do you feel that you would now like to read the rest of the book?
Write some sentences to explain your answer.

A Smuggler's Song

If you wake at midnight and hear a horse's feet,
Don't go drawing back the blind, or looking at the street,
Them that ask no questions isn't told a lie.
Watch the wall, my darling, while the Gentlemen go by!
      Five and twenty ponies,
      Trotting through the dark –
      Brandy for the Parson,
      'Baccy for the Clerk;
      Laces for the lady; letters for a spy,
And watch the wall, my darling, while the Gentlemen go by!

Running round the woodlump if you chance to find
Little barrels, roped and tarred, all full of brandy-wine;
Don't you shout to come and look, nor take 'em for your play.
Put the brushwood back again – and they'll be gone next day!

If you see the stable-door setting open wide;
If you see a tired horse lying down inside;
If your mother mends a coat cut about and tore;
If the lining's wet and warm – don't you ask no more!

If you meet King George's men, dressed in blue and red,
You be careful what you say, and mindful what is said.
If they call you 'pretty maid', and chuck you 'neath the chin,
Don't you tell where no one is, nor yet where no one's been!

Knocks and footsteps round the house – whistles after dark –
You've no call for running out till the house-dogs bark.
Trusty's here and Pitcher's here, and see how dumb they lie –
They don't fret to follow when the Gentlemen go by!

If you do as you've been told, likely there's a chance,
You'll be given a dainty doll, all the way from France,
With a cap of Valenciennes, and a velvet hood –
A present from the Gentlemen, along o' being good!
        Five and twenty ponies,
        Trotting through the dark –
        Brandy for the Parson,
        'Baccy for the Clerk.
Them that asks no questions isn't told a lie –
Watch the wall, my darling, while the Gentlemen go by!

Rudyard Kipling

Do you remember?

Write the correct answer to each question.

1. At what time do the horses go by?
   a) The horses go by at midday.
   b) The horses go by at midnight.

2. How many ponies are used?
   a) 25 ponies are used.
   b) 52 ponies are used.

3. What is hidden under the brushwood?
   a) Tobacco is hidden under the brushwood.
   b) Brandy-wine is hidden under the brushwood.

4. What are the colours of the uniforms of the King's men?
   a) The King's men wear red and green uniforms.
   b) The King's men wear blue and red uniforms.

5. How many dogs are kept to guard the house?
   a) There are two guard dogs.
   b) There is one guard dog.

More to think about

Write a sentence to answer each question.

1. Where do you imagine the story of this poem is set?
2. Who is the speaker talking to? How can you tell whether they are male or female?
3. What is the person being told?
4. Who are "the Gentlemen" and who are "King George's men"?
5. Why do you think that the brandy-wine will be gone by the next day?
6. Why do you think mother is mending a coat with a wet lining?
7. Whose dogs are Trusty and Pitcher? Why don't they bark?
8. What is meant by "watch the wall" in this poem?

Now try these

1. Make a list of the items mentioned in the poem that have been smuggled.
2. Is the poet on the side of the smugglers or King George's men? How can you tell?
3. Imagine that you live in a little fishing village, several hundred years ago, and your father has asked you to join the smugglers tonight for the first time. Describe how you are feeling and what happens as you lead the horses down to the beach on this dark, still night.

Sedna the Great Inuit Goddess

The Inuit (once called Eskimos) depend largely on the sea for their food. Their great goddess is a sea spirit. This is her story.

Long, long ago, two giants gave birth to a baby girl who was named Sedna. She did not remain a small baby for long. She had such an enormous appetite and consumed so much food that she quickly grew very big indeed. Any joints of meat that she saw she would grab and gluttonously gobble up. Keeping the child fed was becoming an increasingly desperate task, causing the two old giants terrible anguish.

One night as the giants lay sleeping, they felt great pains in their legs. They awoke, and to their horror and utter astonishment realised that Sedna was trying to eat them!

"Enough, enough! We have had enough," they said. They got up, grabbed their monster child, and forced her into their umaik (hunting canoe). In the darkness they paddled out to sea, and when they were a great distance from the shore, pushed Sedna overboard into the dark, icy-cold waters of the northern ocean.

But Sedna's hands rose from the waves and she grabbed onto the side of the boat. Fearing for their lives, afraid that she would overturn the vessel, they knew they had to do something quickly. The giants grabbed for their hunting knives and slashed at Sedna's hands. As, one by one, her fingers fell into the sea they became swallowed up by the waves and turned into the creatures of the deep we know today – seals, walruses, whales and the huge shoals of fish, all of which are the food on which the Inuit people have survived for generation after generation.

But what of poor Sedna? Well, she sank to the bottom of the sea where to this very day she lives as the goddess of the sea and all its creatures.

Do you remember?

Read these sentences about the story.
Write 'true', 'false' or 'can't tell' for each one.

1. Sedna was born to two ordinary Inuit.

2. She had two sisters.

3. Sedna grew very quickly.

4. She had an enormous appetite.

5. She even tried to eat her own parents!

6. Her grandmother said she was such a difficult child because her parents hadn't been strict enough.

7. Her parents put her in a boat and hoped they wouldn't see her again.

8. Her parents took her out to sea and threw her overboard.

9. She sank to the bottom of the sea and became the goddess of all the sea creatures.

More to think about

1. Write a sentence to answer each question.
   a) Why was it so hard to keep Sedna fed?
   b) What made Sedna's parents realise they needed to do something drastic?
   c) How do we know that the "baby" had become very big by the time her parents took her out to sea?
   d) Why is Sedna now the great goddess of the Inuit?

2. Copy this extract from the passage. Use different words in place of the eight words printed in bold, without changing the meaning.

   Long, long ago, two giants gave birth to a baby girl who was named Sedna. She did not **remain** a small baby for long. She had such an **enormous** appetite and **consumed** so much food that she quickly grew very big indeed. Any joints of meat that she saw she would grab and **gluttonously** gobble up. Keeping the child fed was becoming an **increasingly desperate** task, causing the two old giants terrible **anguish**.

   One night as the giants lay sleeping, they felt great pains in their legs. They awoke, and to their horror and utter **astonishment** realised that Sedna was trying to eat them!

Now try these

1. Write a summary of the story in your own words. Your summary should be no more than 50 words.
2. The action of the two giants was a dramatic one. Describe how you think they must have felt on their outward journey, and then on their return journey.
3. The Inuit live in the inhospitable white wilderness of the Arctic wastes of Northern Canada. Write a report about what you think life is like for the Inuit, the problems and the pleasures. If you can, find a reference book to help you before you start; if not, just use your imagination.
4. How did this story leave you feeling? Write a review of the story explaining your reactions and say if you would recommend it to others.

From a Railway Carriage

Faster than fairies, faster than witches,
Bridges and houses, hedges and ditches;
And charging along like troops in a battle,
All through the meadows the horses and cattle;
All of the sights of the hill and the plain
Fly as thick as driving rain;
And ever again, in the wink of an eye,
Painted stations whistle by.

Here is a child who clambers and scrambles,
All by himself and gathering brambles;
Here is a tramp who stands and gazes;
And there is a green for stringing the daisies!
Here is a cart run away in the road
Lumping along with a man and a load;
And here is a mill and there is a river;
Each a glimpse and gone for ever!

Robert Louis Stevenson

Do you remember?

Write a sentence to answer each question.

1. What animals are in the meadow as the train passes?
2. What is described as "painted"?
3. What is the child collecting?
4. Who stands and watches the train pass by?
5. What can be seen on the road?

More to think about

1. Write some sentences to answer each question.
   a) What clues can you find in the poem that show it was written many years ago?
   b) How does the poet describe the speed of the train?
   c) What phrase does he use to show that a large number of sights fly past very quickly?

2. Write down these words and then find a word in the poem that rhymes with each of them.
   a) witches
   b) cattle
   c) rain
   d) eye
   e) scrambles
   f) gazes
   g) road

3. Now write two extra rhyming words of your own to go with the pairs you have just written.

Now try these

1. Did you enjoy this poem? What is it about the poem that you liked most? Give your reasons.

2. How does the way the poet has written this famous poem make you think of a train rushing along a track?

3. Choose a different way of travelling. Think carefully about the sounds made by the vehicle and how it makes you feel.
   Make a list of the words and phrases you think of.

4. Going on any long journey is exciting. Write a poem about a journey you have been on. Use your list of words to help, if you like.

The Snow Spider

After tea Mr Griffiths vanished into his workshop. His work-load of farm repairs seemed to increase rather than diminish, and Gwyn often wondered if it was his father's way of avoiding conversation.

He thought, impatiently, of the drawer in his room, while his mother chattered about Christmas and the cockerel. Then, excusing himself with a quick hug, Gwyn left his mother to talk to the cat and, trying not to show an unnatural enthusiasm for bed, crossed the passage and climbed the stairs slowly, but two at a time.

His bedroom door was open and there appeared to be a soft glow within. On entering the room Gwyn froze. There were shadows on the wall; seven helmeted figures, motionless beside his bed. He turned, fearfully, to locate the source of light. It came from behind a row of toy spacemen standing on the chest of drawers. Gwyn breathed a sigh of relief and approached the spacemen.

The silver spider had climbed out of the drawer. It was glowing in the dark.

Gwyn brushed his toys aside and hesitantly held out his hand to the spider. It crawled into his open palm and, gently, he raised it closer to his face. The spider's touch was icy cold, and yet the glow that it shed on his face had a certain strange warmth that seemed to penetrate every part of his body.

He held the spider for several minutes, admiring the exquisite pattern on its back and wondering whether there was more to the tiny creature than a superficial beauty… had the extraordinary spider come from a place beyond this world?

Replacing the spider in the drawer, Gwyn went downstairs to fetch a book. When he returned the glow came from the bedpost and, deciding that he had no need for an electric light, he sat on his bed and read his book beside the spider. It was an exceptional sensation, reading by spiderlight.

Jenny Nimmo

Do you remember?

Copy these sentences. Fill each gap.

1. After tea Mr Griffiths went to his _____.
2. Gwyn left his mother talking to the _____.
3. When he reached his _____ he found the door open.
4. There were _____ on the wall.
5. The spider was _____ in the dark.
6. It felt _____ when he touched it.
7. He held the spider for several _____.
8. He sat on his _____ and read his book.

More to think about

1. Write a sentence to answer each question.
   a) What made Gwyn think his father wanted to avoid conversation?
   b) What does the author mean when she says Gwyn did not want to show "an unnatural enthusiasm for bed"?
   c) When Gwyn reached his room he saw the shadows of seven helmeted figures. What was his reaction?
   d) What were they really?
   e) What, apart from its glow, was unusual about Gwyn's spider?
   f) What does "it was an exceptional sensation" mean?

2. Use a dictionary to help you to match each of these definitions to a word in the grid. The first one has been done to help you.
a) get smaller   C1
b) disappear
c) extremely beautiful
d) get bigger
e) not moving
f) get inside
g) feeling
h) exceptional
i) not very deep

	A	B	C
1	vanish	increase	diminish
2	motionless	exquisite	superficial
3	penetrate	extraordinary	sensation

Now try these

1. Write a short description of each of the three characters in the passage: Gwyn, Mr Griffiths and Mrs Griffiths. Think especially about the clues you get about their personalities from the passage. What can you tell about the relationship between Gwyn and his father?

2. Where do you think the spider came from? Write some sentences to explain how you think it might have got its unusual features.

3. What do you think happened in the end? Make notes of how you think the story might finish.

4. Although Gwyn wasn't frightened of spiders, many people are. Others are scared by different small creatures, like mice or rats or snakes. You might be worried by something quite different, like thunderstorms or the dark. Say what frightens you the most, try to explain why, and describe how you feel when you are frightened.

Ginger

In this extract from *Black Beauty*, Ginger tells her friend, Black Beauty, some of the cruelty she endured when she was younger.

"I never had any one, horse or man, that was kind to me, or that I cared to please; for in the first place I was taken from my mother as soon as I was weaned, and put with a lot of other young colts; none of them cared for me, and I cared for none of them. There was no kind master like yours to look after me, and to talk to me, and bring me nice things to eat. The man that had care of us never gave me a kind word in my life. I do not mean that he ill-used me, but that he did not care for us one bit further than to see that we had plenty to eat and shelter in the winter.

"A footpath ran through our field and very often the great boys passing through would fling stones to make us gallop. I was never hit, but one fine colt was badly cut in the face, and I should think it would be a scar for life. We did not care for them, but of course it made us more wild, and we settled it in our minds that boys were our enemies.

"We had some very good times in the free meadows, galloping up and down and chasing each other round and round the field; then standing still under the shade of the trees. But then it came to breaking in, that was a bad time for me; several men came to catch me, and when at last they closed me in one corner of the field, one caught me by the forelock, another caught me by the nose, and held it so tight I could hardly breathe; then another took me under jaw in his hard hand and wrenched my mouth open, and so by force they got on the halter and the bar into my mouth; then one dragged me along by the halter, another flogging behind, and this was the first experience I had of men's kindness, it was all force; they did not give me a chance to know what they wanted.

"There was a strong, tall bold man; they called him Samson, and he used to boast that he had never found a horse that could throw him. There was no gentleness in him, but only hardness, a hard voice, a hard eye, a hard hand, and I felt from the first that what he wanted was to wear all the spirit out of me, and just make me a quiet, humble, obedient piece of horse-flesh. 'Horse-flesh!' Yes, that is all that he thought about," and Ginger stamped her foot as if the very thought of him made her angry.

She went on: "I could never quite tell how it came about; he had only just mounted me on the training ground when something I did put him out of temper, and he chucked me hard with the rein. The new bit was very painful, and I reared up suddenly, which angered him still more, and he began to flog me. I felt my whole spirit set against him, and I began to kick and plunge, and rear as I had never done before, and we had a regular fight; for a long time he stuck to the saddle and punished me cruelly with his whip and spurs, but my blood was thoroughly up, and I cared for nothing he could do if only I could get him off. At last, after a terrible struggle, I threw him off backwards. I heard him fall heavily on the turf, and without looking behind me, I galloped off to the other end of the field; there I turned round and saw my persecutor slowly rising from the ground and going into the stable."

Anna Sewell

Do you remember?

Write the correct answer to each question.

1. When was Ginger taken from her mother?
   a) She was taken from her mother at birth.
   b) She was taken from her mother as soon as she was weaned.

2. Did she get on well with the other young horses?
   a) Yes, Ginger was pleased to be with the other colts.
   b) No, Ginger didn't like the other colts.

3. Why didn't she like the boys who came through her field?
   a) The boys threw stones at the horses.
   b) The boys made noises to frighten the horses.

4. Was Ginger's breaking-in a good time for her?
   a) No, the men were cruel to her.
   b) Yes, the men broke her in gently.

More to think about

1. Write a sentence to answer each question.
   a) Ginger said her master did not ill-use her, but he did not care for her. What does she mean by this?
   b) Why did she think all boys were her enemy?
   c) When, as a young horse, was Ginger most content?
   d) In the third paragraph she says: "this was the first experience I had of men's kindness". She was being sarcastic. What does she really mean?
   e) Why was the man who was trying to break-in Ginger called Samson?
   f) Why was she so upset that he described her as "horse-flesh"?

2. One word in each sentence is not correct. Write each sentence correctly.
   a) Ginger wasn't pleased not to be with her old master.
   b) Ginger and Black Beauty was friends.
   c) The boys passing threw the field threw stones.
   d) Ginger run around in the meadow with the other colts.
   e) She walked off to the end of the field.

Now try these

1. Find these phrases in the last paragraph of the passage. Write in your own words what each one means.
   a) put him out of temper
   b) he chucked me hard
   c) my blood was thoroughly up
   d) I cared for nothing he could do
   e) my persecutor

2. Except in stories like this, animals can't speak, but like us they can feel pain. They also learn to have feelings about people, so they can think. Imagine that you are an animal. Write about your life and feelings. Tell your readers about:
   • where you are kept
   • what you are fed
   • whether you have other animal friends
   • how your owners treat you
   • anything you really wish could be changed.

Horses of the Sun

Phaeton, the son of Helios, the Greek sun god, begged his father to allow him to drive his chariot for just one day. He was desperate to impress his friends on Earth, none of whom believed he was the son of a god. Eventually his father relented.

"But whatever you do," he said sternly, "do not try to guide the horses. They know the path and, if you do not bother them, they will ride in an arc across the sky, until they reach the safety of the stables in the West."

He had time to say no more. The great golden courtyard gates swung open. Light began to climb into the dark sky and the restless horses leaped into the waiting blackness.

Helios watched as the wheels and the hooves made splinters of light which surrounded the chariot like a ball of fire.

Phaeton held on tightly to the reins. The chariot thundered into the sky with a speed that made his cloak stream out behind him. The wind lifted his hair and his breath came in gasps.

Gradually, though, he relaxed and he began to enjoy the power and the swiftness of his flight. He looked over the side and thought of the people woken by the rays from the sun chariot. He laughed aloud when he thought of the power he had to control people's lives.

"Soon I shall be over my village," he thought happily, but when he looked over at the ground below him all he could see were patches of grey, brown and green. He was too far away even to see his village, let alone his house.

In despair he cried, "No one will see that it is me driving the chariot." He gave the reins an angry tug and steered the great horses away from their path in the sky. Nearer to Earth they swooped. The stallions gathered speed and hurtled downwards. Too late, Phaeton remembered his father's warning, and he tried desperately to stop the furious flight. The horses, sensing that they were no longer controlled, galloped faster and faster. Their flaming nostrils sent fire licking onto the earth and sparks flew from their hooves. Flames licked buildings, and crops withered and died in the heat. Huge rivers were sucked into the air and only barren, scorched beds remained.

People were in panic. Dust from the parched ground filled their nostrils. Soil crumbled around them. Where were they to turn for help?

Only the father of the gods, Zeus, could help them. Gathering what little they had to offer as gifts, the villagers streamed to his temple and begged for help.

Their pitiful cries soon reached the great god and he looked down with amazement at the devastation. He saw the sun chariot racing in great swirls across the sky, the driver hanging on grimly.

Taking a thunderbolt, Zeus hurled it with great force at the frightened boy. It hit Phaeton and its power sent him spinning out of the chariot. His body twisted in space until it landed, broken, on the Earth.

At a command from Zeus, the horses returned to their proper path. Streaming foam from their bodies made a shimmering haze around them and, as night came, the hidden chariot dissolved into the West and the darkness.

When Phaeton's sisters saw what had happened, they wept and travelled to where he lay. They found his body smashed on a rocky desert and wept bitterly for him.

Zeus saw their sorrow and took pity on them. He changed Phaeton's body into a quiet stream and his sisters' tears into pieces of golden amber, glinting in the sunlight. Slowly, at the edge of the stream, the girls themselves began to change into slender poplar trees which swayed and whispered sorrowfully in the wind.

In this way the cooling blessings of water and shade returned to Earth, and the people were thankful to Zeus for saving them. Phaeton had had what he wanted. He had driven the horses of the sun, but he had not lived to boast about his journey.

**Barrie Wade, Ann Wade
and Maggie Moore**

Do you remember?

Copy these sentences. Fill each gap.

1. _____ was the son of Helios.

2. Helios was the Greek _____ god.

3. Phaeton wanted to be allowed to drive his father's _____.

4. Helios warned him not to guide the _____.

5. Phaeton took the chariot too close to his _____.

6. Zeus, the father of the gods, sent a _____ to stop the disaster.

More to think about

1. Read these sentences about the story. Copy them in the right order.

> **The stallions hurtled downwards.**

> **Phaeton begged his father, Helios, to be allowed to drive the chariot.**

> **Phaeton flew over his village, and wanted everyone to see him.**

> **Phaeton was killed.**

> **The flames and heat severely damaged the Earth.**

> **Zeus sent a thunderbolt that threw Phaeton out of the chariot.**

> **Zeus changed Phaeton's body into a cool stream.**

2. Write a sentence to answer each question.
   a) What was Phaeton's main reason for wanting to drive his father's chariot?
   b) What was the chariot really? What clues make you think this?
   c) Why were the ancient people of Greece more likely to have legends about the sun than early people in countries like Britain?
   d) When Phaeton was over his village he said "No one will see that it is me driving the chariot." What does this tell you about him?

3. The authors have used some interestingly descriptive phrases.
   Find in the passage, and copy into your book, how they describe:
   a) the first light of dawn.
   b) what happened to Phaeton after he was hit by the thunderbolt.
   c) Phaeton's sisters' tears.
   d) the poplar trees.

Now try these

1. Write a summary of the events that led to Phaeton's death.
   Your summary should be no more than 60 words.

2. Many myths and legends like this one have a hidden moral, or meaning.
   What do you think is the moral of this story?

3. Adults often ask young people not to do things that may be dangerous or cause problems. Write about something you have done that you had been asked not to, or knew you shouldn't, or wish that you hadn't! Did you learn anything from the experience?

To the RESCUE

Cubs and Brownies to the RESCUE

MORETON: Anglers and conservation volunteers were joined yesterday by Cubs and Brownies from packs in the town to help with the annual spring clean of Prospect Park as part of the RESCUE event.

Moreton Town Council and Friends of Caversham Woods backed the local rivers and environmental clean-up event, along with other local authorities and voluntary groups.

The good news for those taking part was that the volume of rubbish was less than previous years, and down by about half on three years ago when the scheme was launched.

"However, there are still a few local residents who are dumping garden and other refuse within the park," according to a spokeswoman for the environment department at the council. "Recently a large amount of old engine oil was illegally disposed of in a litter bin which could have caused a pollution incident."

The town's mayor, Mr Jack Alaman, who watched the working parties in the park, commented, "The majority of visitors to our park are proud of our town and its park. They do not leave litter or dump rubbish. But you always seem to get a few who spoil it for the many. I am pleased to see so many young people here to help clean up the park. We seek to involve local schools and youth groups in the care of the area, in the hope that the next generation will care for their environment."

Do you remember?

Write a sentence to answer each question.

1. Who were cleaning the park?
2. What was the event called?
3. Was there more or less rubbish this year than last?
4. What was found recently in a litter bin?
5. Who was pleased to see so many young people helping?

More to think about

1. Read these sentences about the newspaper report.
   Write 'true' or 'not true' for each one.
   a) The Cubs and Brownies helped the anglers and conservation volunteers.
   b) The event takes place every six months.
   c) Some people were cleaning up the river while others worked in the park.
   d) There was more rubbish collected this year than last.
   e) This year there was much less rubbish than three years ago.
   f) Some people drop their garden litter in the park rather than taking it to the refuse dump.
   g) The mayor, Mr Alaman, was pleased with the clean-up.
   h) He said young people leave most of the rubbish so they should clean it up.

2. Write a sentence to answer each question.
   a) Why were so many people prepared to give up their free time to clean up other people's litter?
   b) What do you think is the advantage of having one big RESCUE event each year rather than a few people going out each weekend?
   c) Can you think of reasons why the amount of litter has been down each year?
   d) What does the mayor mean when he says, "But you always get a few who spoil it for the many"?

Now try these

1. Design a poster to advertise this event. Think carefully about the wording you use on your poster to persuade people to join in.

2. Write a letter to your Member of Parliament saying how you would suggest dealing with people who continue to dump their rubbish and waste in public places. Explain your reasons.

3. Huge amounts of money are spent on putting things into packages. These boxes and wrappings create an enormous amount of rubbish. Write a sentence to answer each question.
    a) Why do manufacturers put so many items in expensive packaging?
    b) Who pays for the packaging in the end?
    c) Easter eggs have expensive packaging and so do many toys. How would you feel if you were given presents that didn't have colourful boxes?
    d) What would be the disadvantages if supermarkets sold items like sugar or butter or eggs without packaging?
    e) Which items that you use at home could be sold without packaging?